H 1005

HANON

The Virtuoso Pianist

Part II – Scales and Arpeggios

EDITED BY
ROBERT HEATH

THE
F·J·H
MUSIC
COMPANY
INC.

Frank J. Hackinson

Production: Frank J. Hackinson
Production Coordinator: Satish Bhakta
Engraving: Tempo Music Press, Inc.
Printer: Tempo Music Press, Inc.

THE
F·J·H
MUSIC
COMPANY
I N C.
Frank J. Hackinson

ISBN-13: 978-1-56939-025-2

HANON: THE VIRTUOSO PIANIST

TABLE OF CONTENTS

ABOUT CHARLES-LOUIS HANON

ithout the success of *The Virtuoso Pianist*, Charles-Louis Hanon would be all but forgotten today. Few details are known about his life, even some of the meager published information about him has recently been shown to be erroneous.

Hanon was born on July 2, 1819 in the village of Renescure, France near Dunkerque. It is uncertain where or with whom he received his musical training, but the focus of his studies was a career in church music. In 1846 he was appointed organist and choir director at the Eglise Saint-Joseph in the town of Boulogne-sur-Mer. Seven years later, he left the post under dubious circumstances and spent the rest of his life in Boulogne teaching piano and voice, and publishing his own music.

A lifelong bachelor, Hanon lived with his brother François and a teacher named Louis Légier. His obituary remembers him as a generous, religious man who lived out his life in the shadow of the church until his death from pneumonia on March 19, 1900.

In addition to *The Virtuoso Pianist*, Hanon wrote both a piano method and an organ method, and compiled a collection of piano literature *(Extraits de chefs-d'oevres des grands maitres)*. His musical compositions include a wide variety of piano music and music for voice.

The 1874 edition of F.J. Fetis' *Biographie des Musiciens* devotes much of its entry on Hanon describing his curious method book on accompanying worship titled *New System, practical and popular, for learning to accompany all plainchant at sight ... without knowing music and without the necessity of consulting a teacher.* The method was designed for use in churches with scarce musical resources and was so successful that in 1867, the Pope wrote Hanon a congratulatory letter and named him an honorary *maestro compositore* of the Accademia di Santa Cecilia in Rome.

The Virtuoso Pianist first appeared in 1873 and won a silver medal at the Exposition Universelle in 1878. At the time of Hanon's death in 1900, the book was in use throughout Europe and the United States. Since then, it has become one of the standards of piano technique.

THE VIRTUOSO PIANIST
PART II – SCALES AND ARPEGGIOS

harles-Louis Hanon's *The Virtuoso Pianist (Le Pianiste-virtuose)* is one of the few 19th-century piano technique methods still in regular use. Concise in its presentation (unlike most of its contemporaries), *The Virtuoso Pianist* is divided into three sections: Part I – exercises for five fingers, Part II – scales and arpeggios, and Part III – advanced technical exercises.

Hanon intended his exercises to be introduced after approximately the first year of study. His objective was to develop the fingers equally and the hands uniformly. In his teaching, Hanon observed that many students displayed an insufficiently developed left hand, and that the fourth and fifth fingers of both hands were weak. He believed that *"…if the five fingers of both hands were trained absolutely equally, they would be prepared to execute anything for the piano. The only question remaining would be that of fingering, which could be readily solved."*

Part II – Scales and Arpeggios introduces the core of piano technique. Part II begins with a continuation of the exercises found in Part I and gradually introduces exercises designed to prepare the student for playing scales, including thumb-under exercises. The twelve major scales with their harmonic and melodic minor scales are then introduced in order of the circle of fifths. Major and minor arpeggios are presented in the same fashion. Chromatic scales and arpeggios of the diminished seventh and dominant seventh are also covered in Part II.

The Virtuoso Pianist exercises concentrate on the physical and technical aspect of piano playing. Yet the mental and musical aspects of piano playing must not be ignored in the pursuit of technical achievement. The teacher should encourage the student's concentration and listening as he or she plays these exercises.

ABOUT THE FJH CLASSIC EDITIONS

JH Classic Editions is one of the finest classical keyboard series in print. Each book has been thoroughly researched and newly engraved. Every effort has been made to enhance the pianist's understanding and enjoyment of the music.

The scholarship, practicality, and typographical layout of these editions make them some of the best available.

ABOUT THE EDITOR

obert Heath has performed throughout the United States as well as in Mexico and Europe as soloist and accompanist on organ and harpsichord. He holds degrees in music theory from Wheaton College Conservatory of Music with graduate studies at the University of Miami. He currently serves as senior organist at Miami's historic Plymouth Congregational Church in Coconut Grove.

In addition, Mr. Heath is the executive director of The Miami Bach Society, which presents acclaimed productions of the masterworks of Bach and his contemporaries. Through his performance and study of 17th and 18th century music, Mr. Heath has become a recognized specialist in the practice of Basso Continuo—the realization of a keyboard part from a figured bass. His skills in this area of Baroque music place him in demand as performer, teacher, and arranger of figured bass.

21

C.L. Hanon

Finger emphasis: 3-4-5

♩ = 60-108

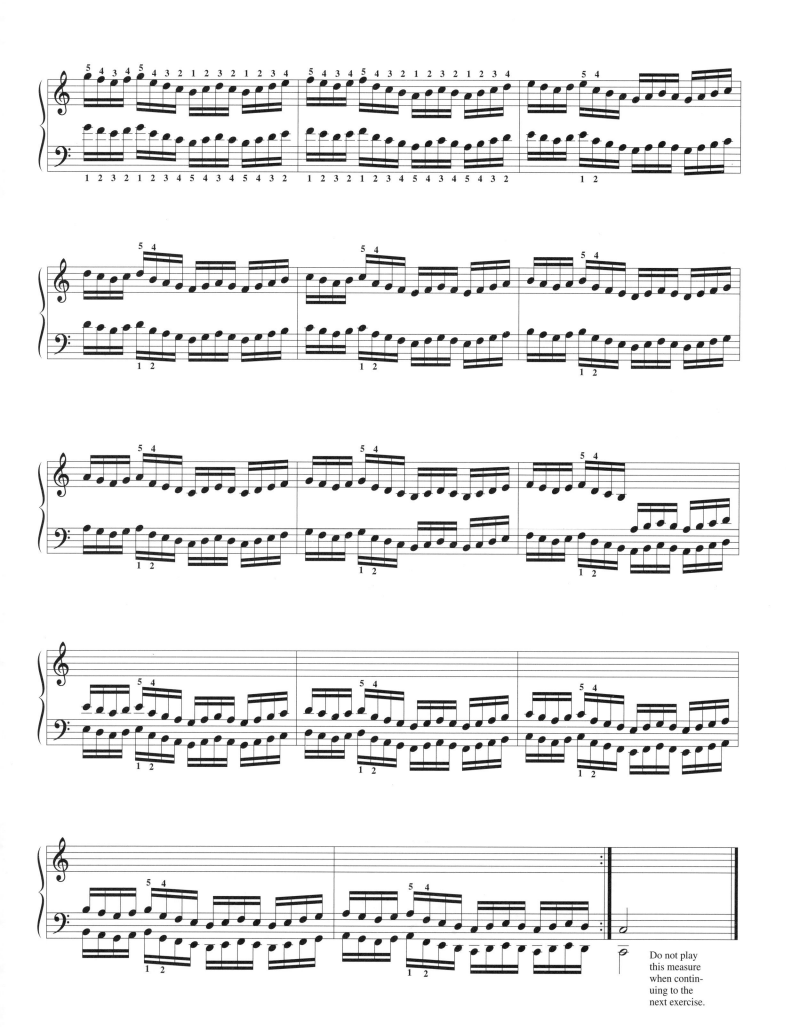

Do not play
this measure
when contin-
uing to the
next exercise.

22

Finger emphasis: 3-4-5

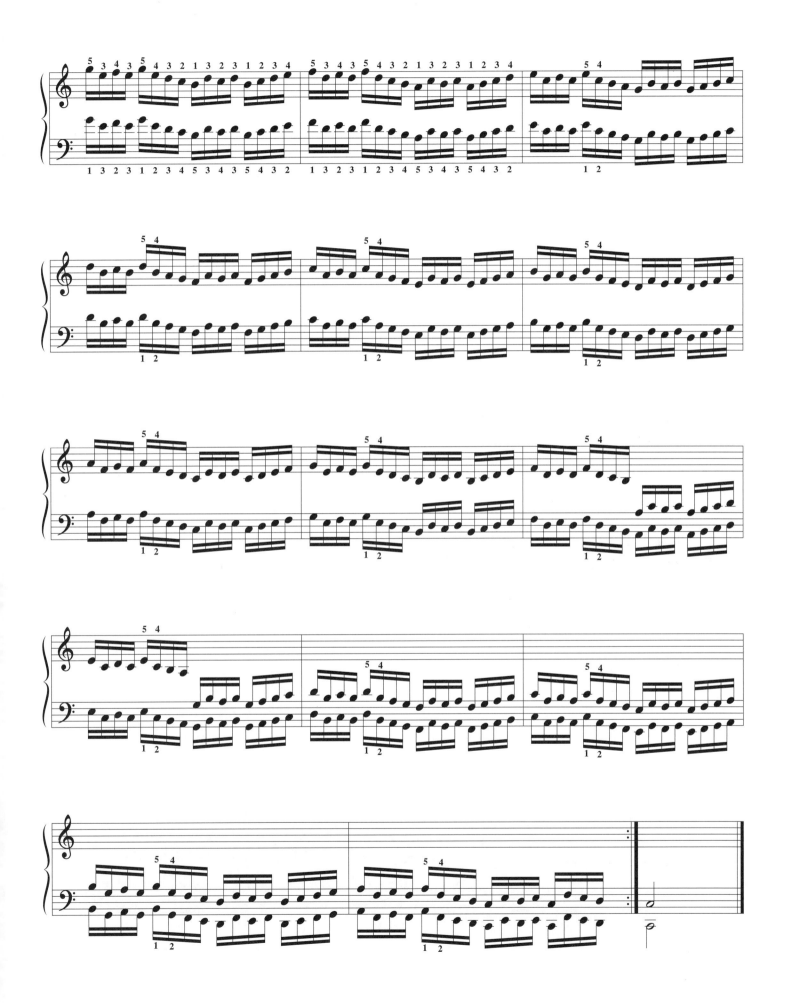

23

Finger emphasis: 3-4-5

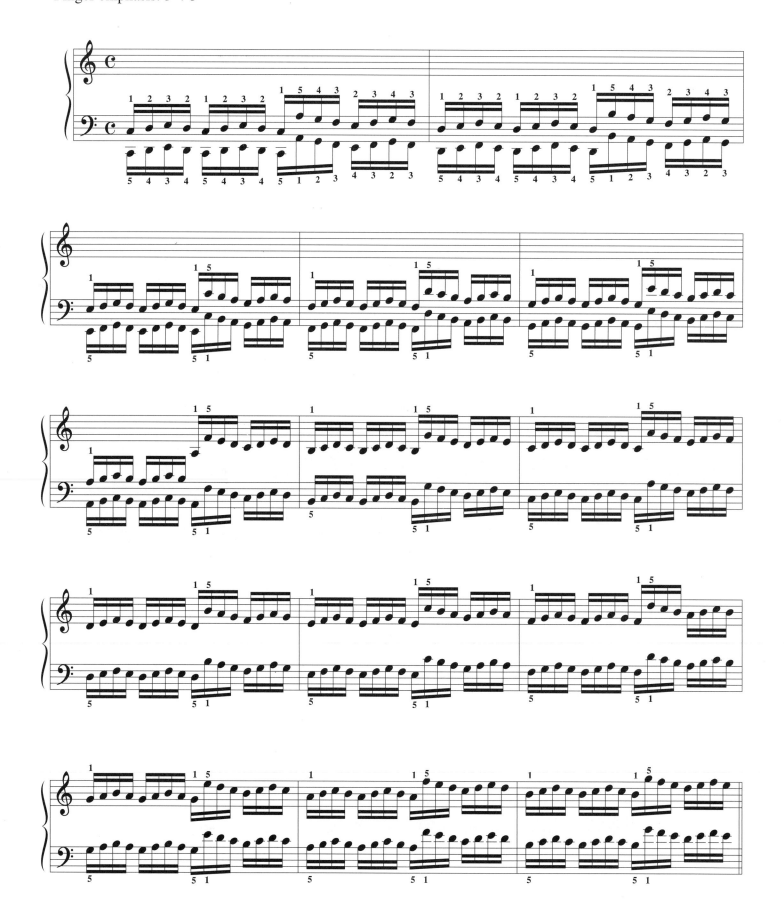

24

Finger emphasis: 3-4-5

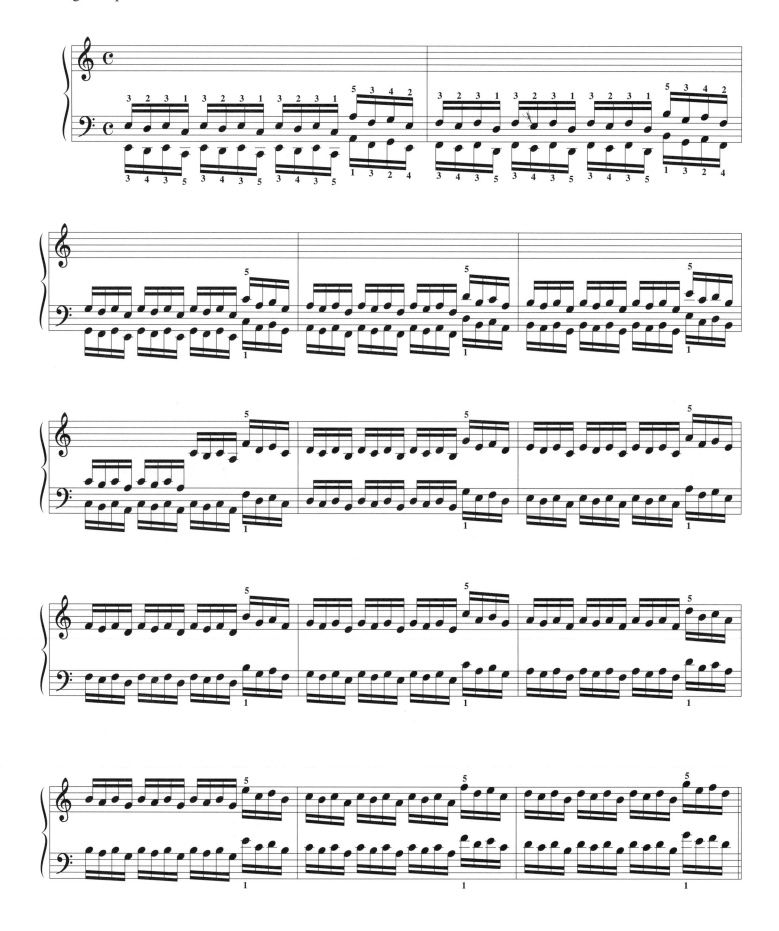

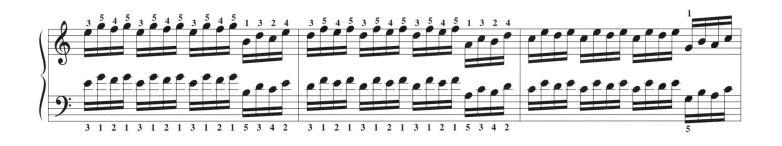

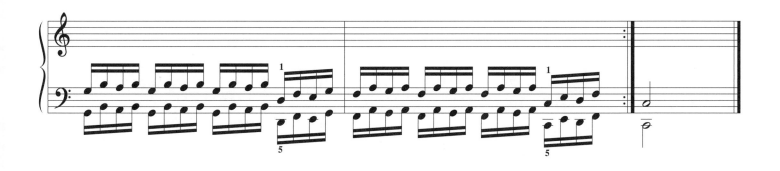

25

Finger emphasis: 1-2-3-4-5

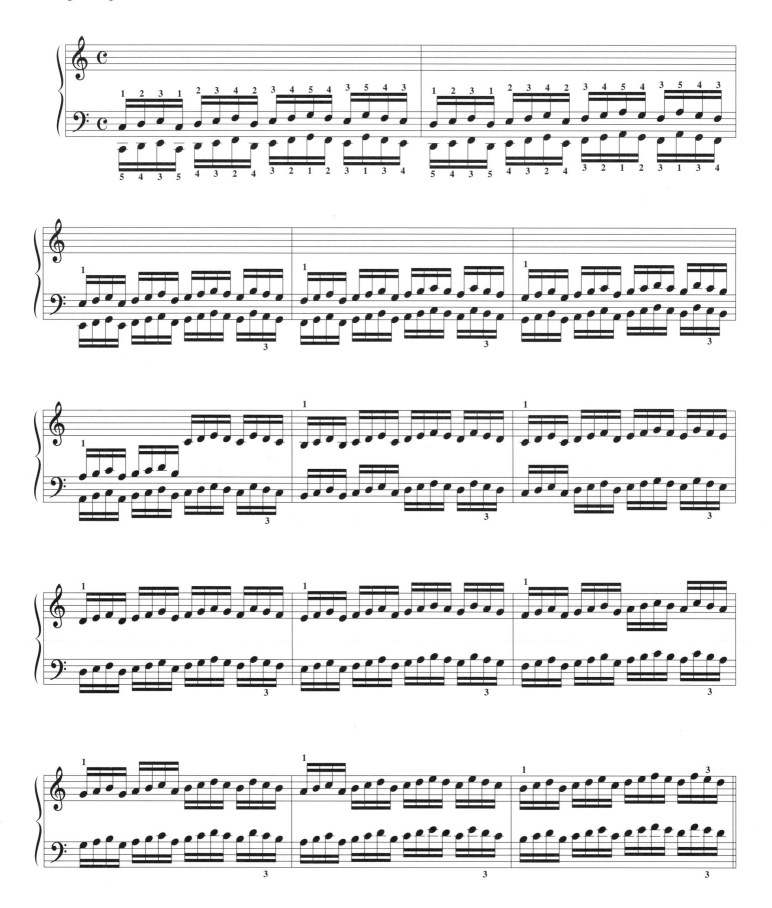

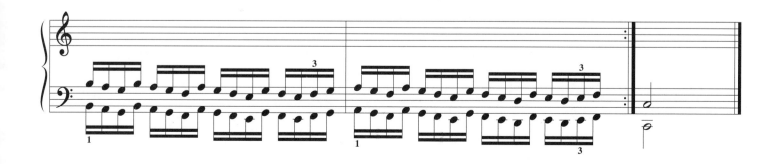

26

Finger emphasis: 1-2-3-4-5

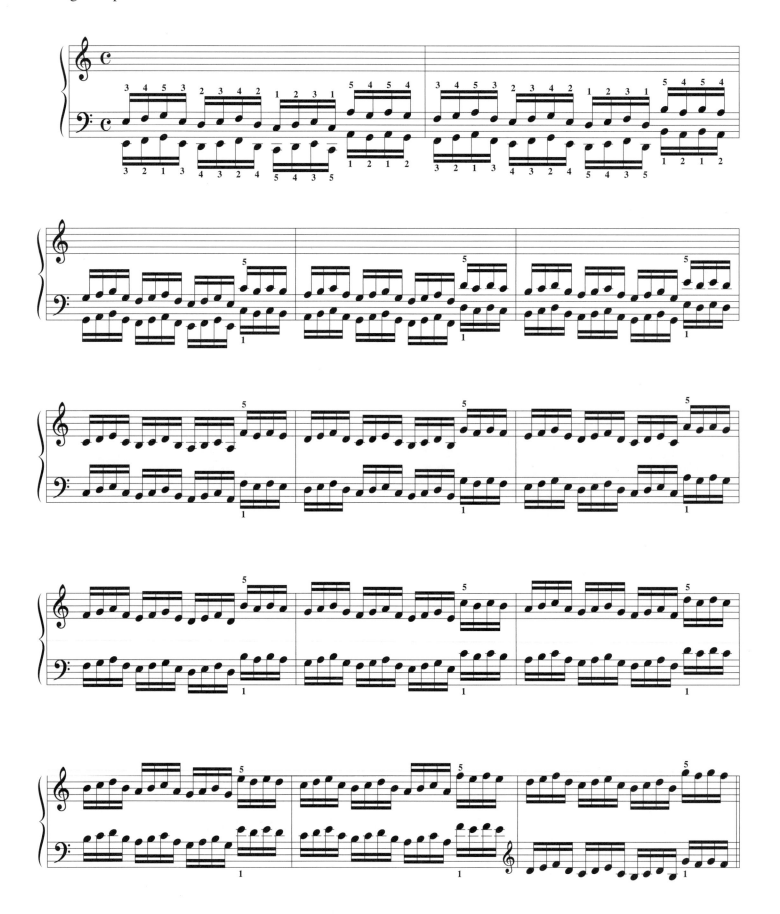

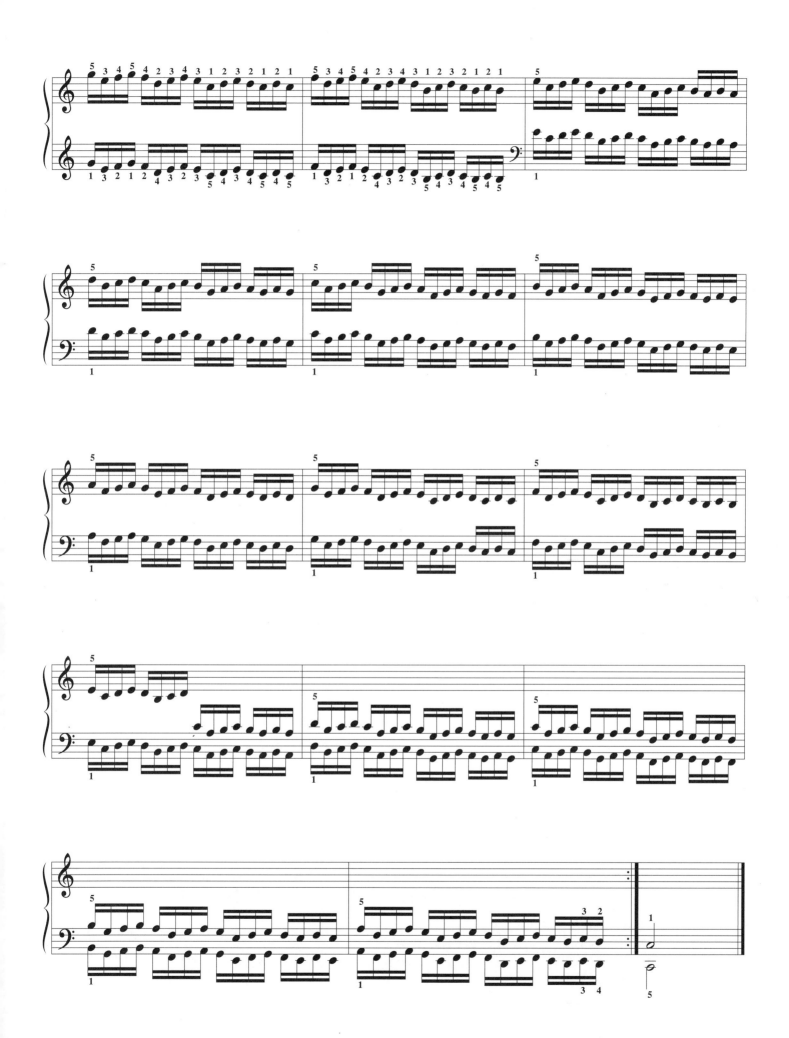

27

Finger emphasis: 1-2-3-4-5; 4-5 (trill preparation)

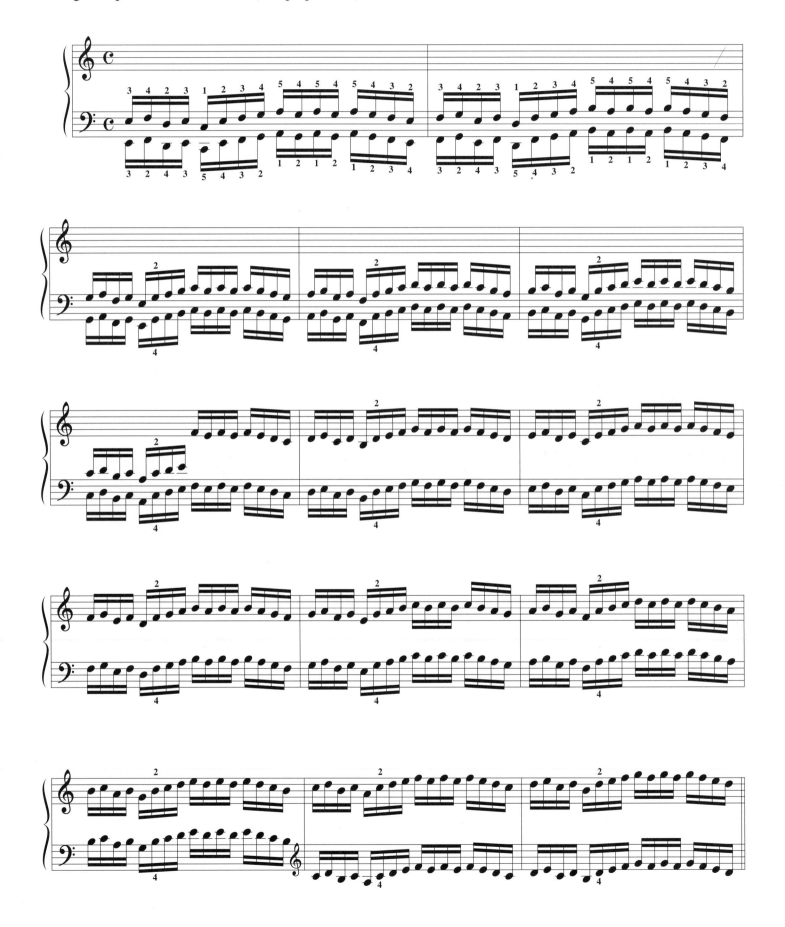

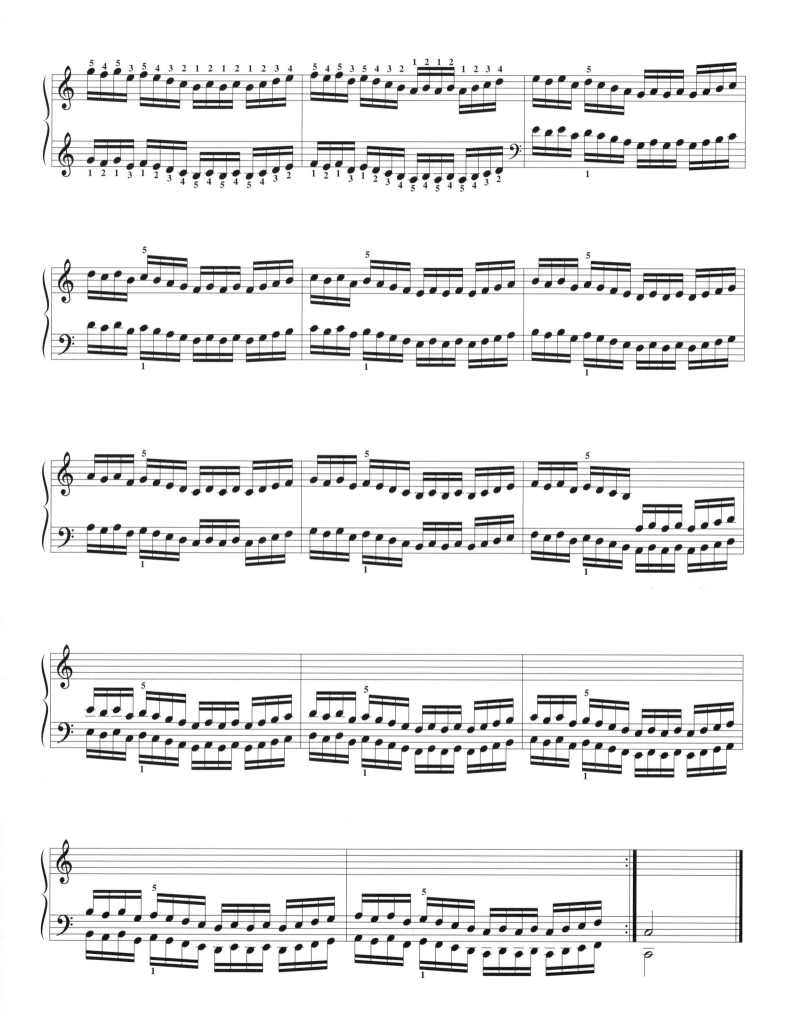

28

Finger emphasis: 3-4-5

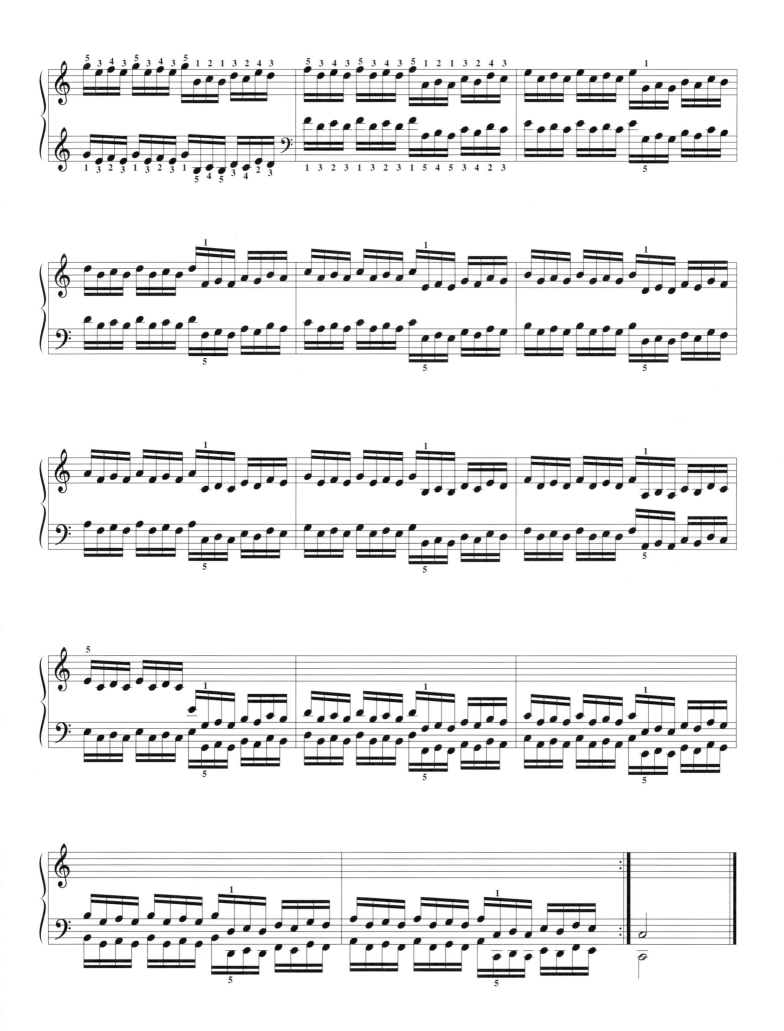

29

Finger emphasis: 1-2-3-4-5 (trill preparation)

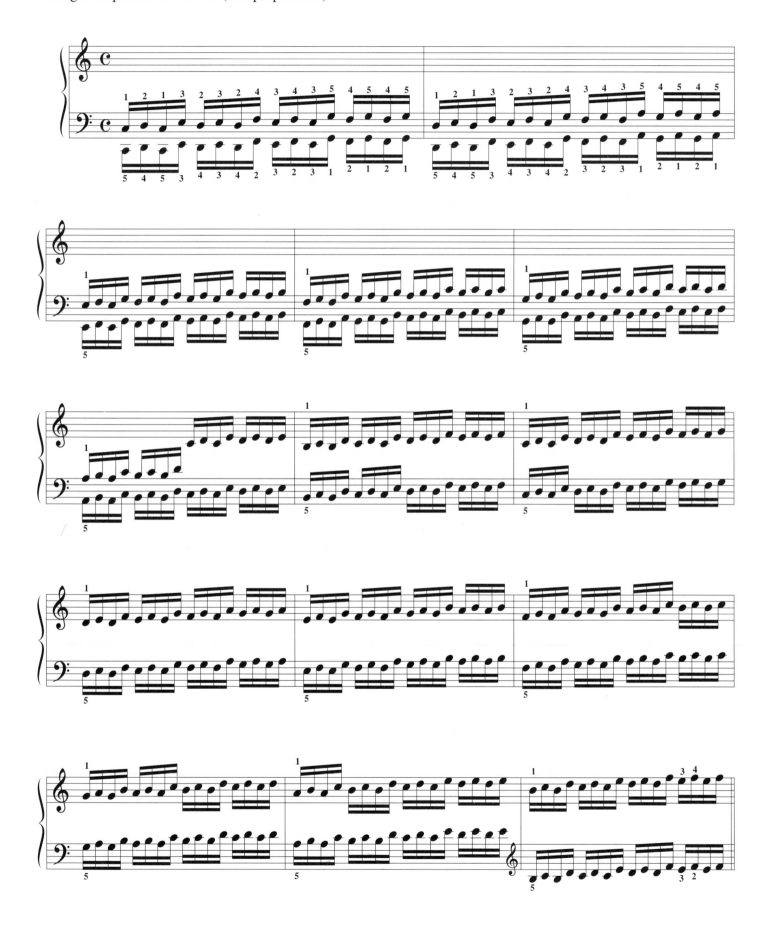

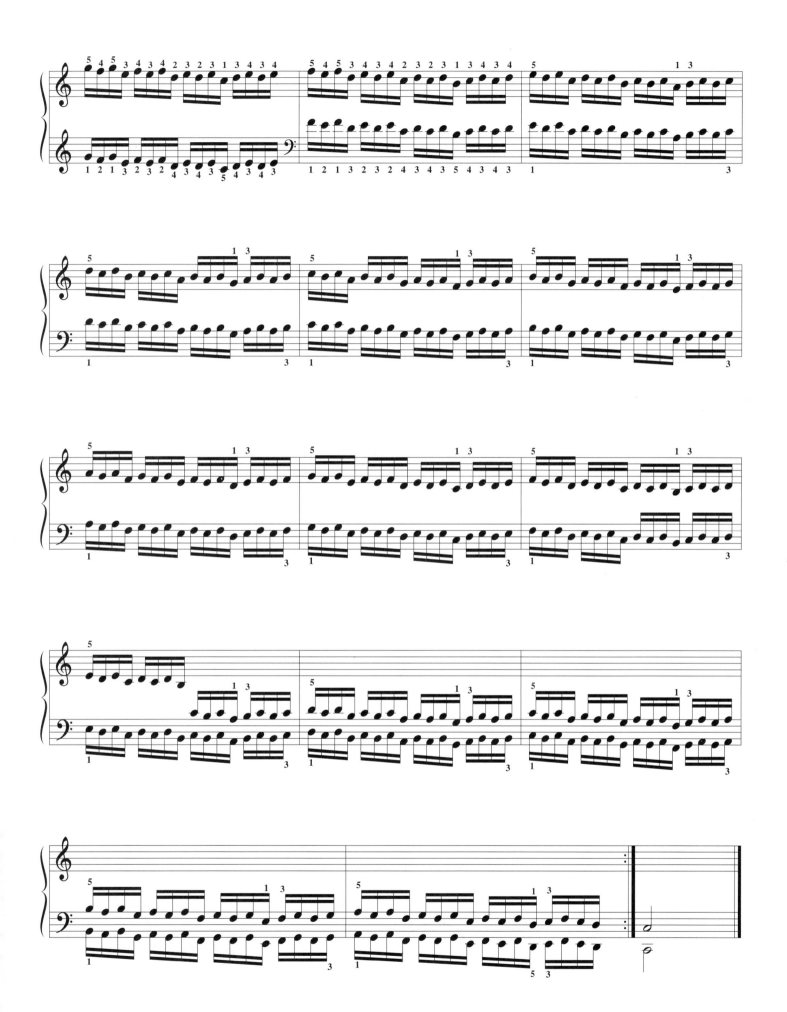

30

Finger emphasis: 1-2, 4-5 (trill preparation)

31

Finger emphasis: 1-2-3-4-5 hand extension

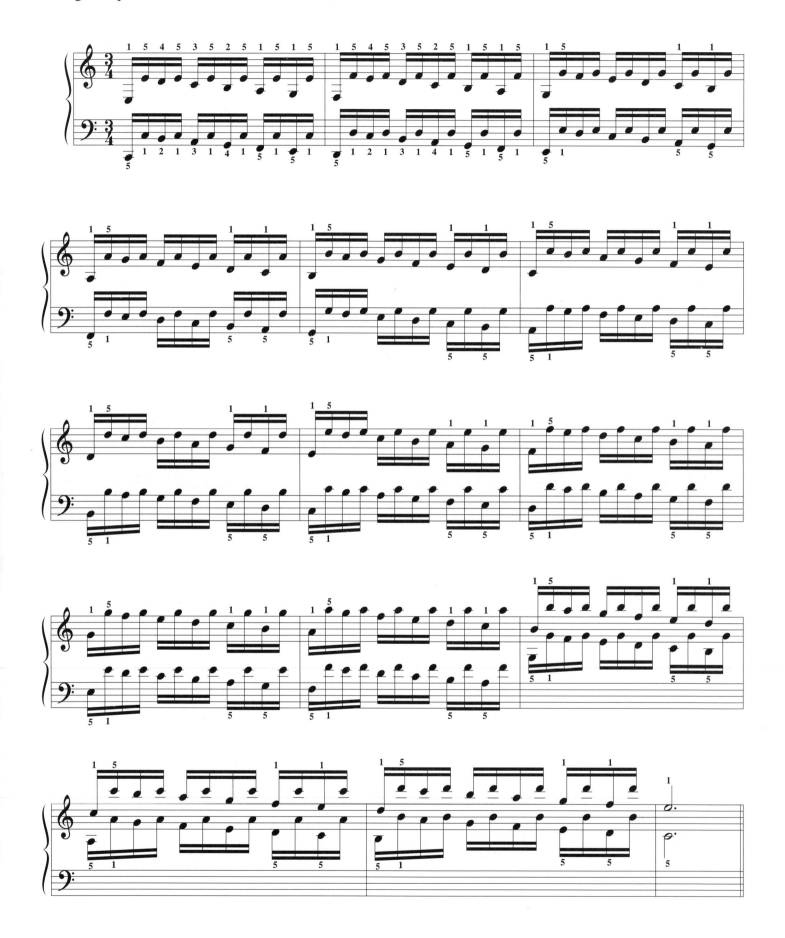

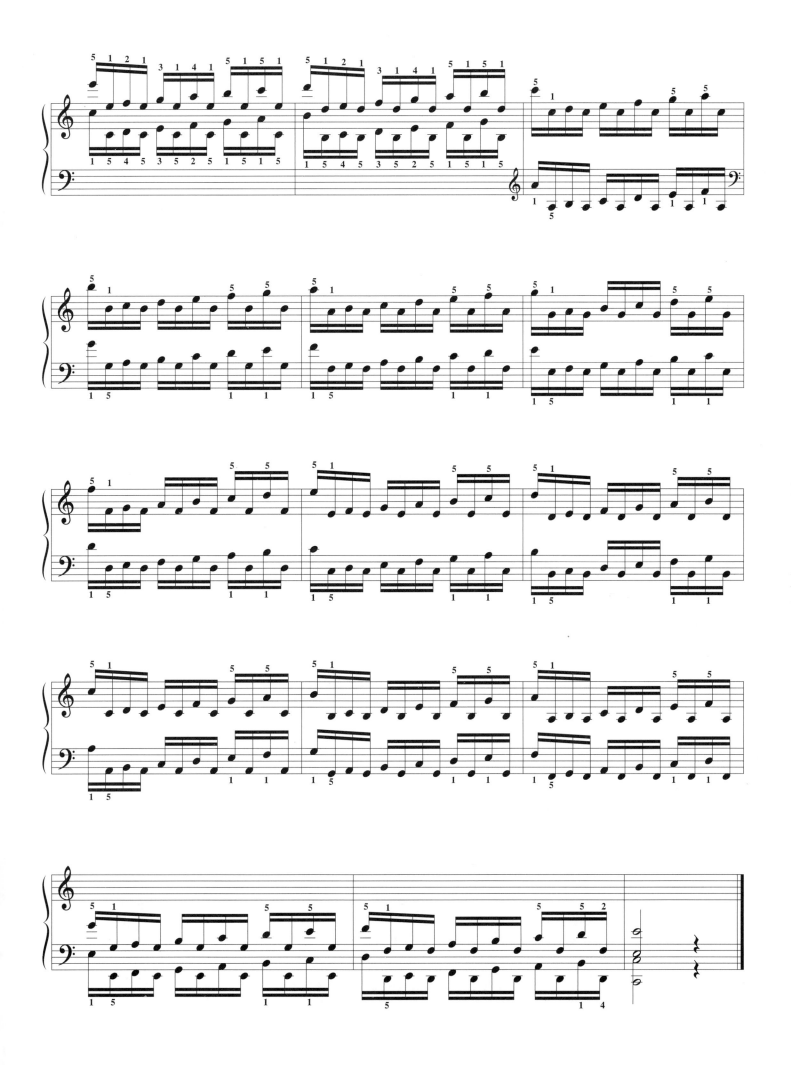

Turning the Thumb Under

32

Turning the thumb under the 2nd finger.

♩ = 40-72

Play this measure 4 times.

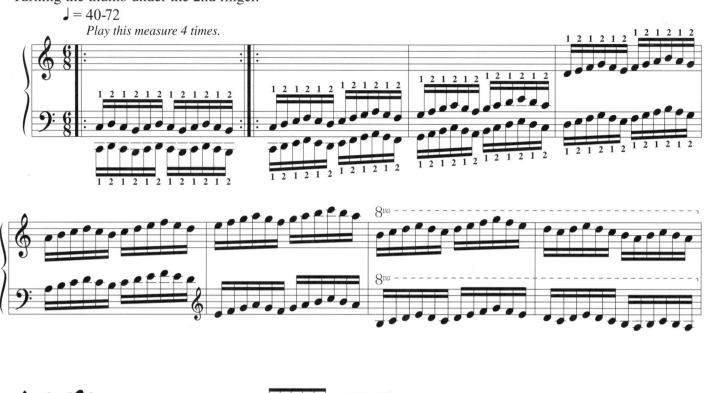

33

Turning the thumb under the 3rd finger.

♩ = 40-72

Play this measure 4 times.

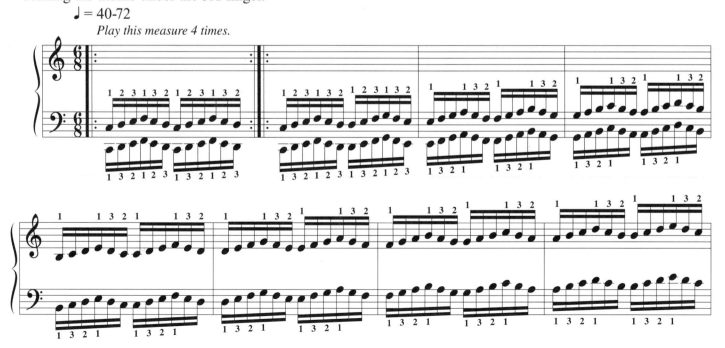

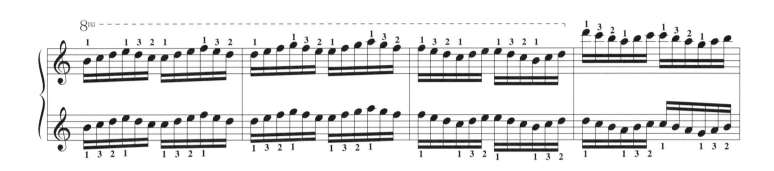

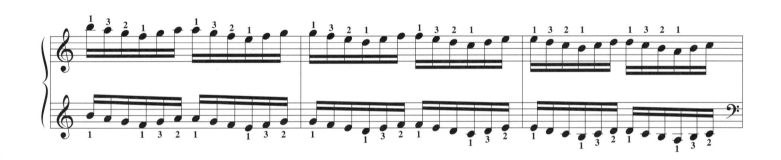

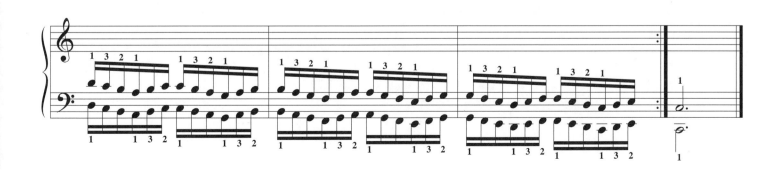

34

Turning the thumb under the 4th finger.

♩ = 60-108

Play this measure 10 times.

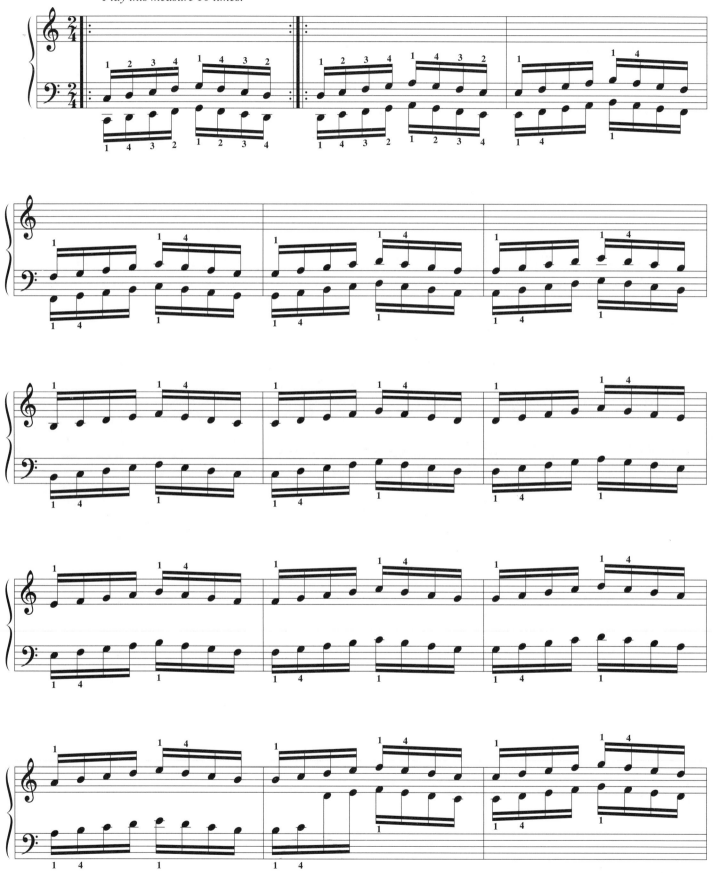

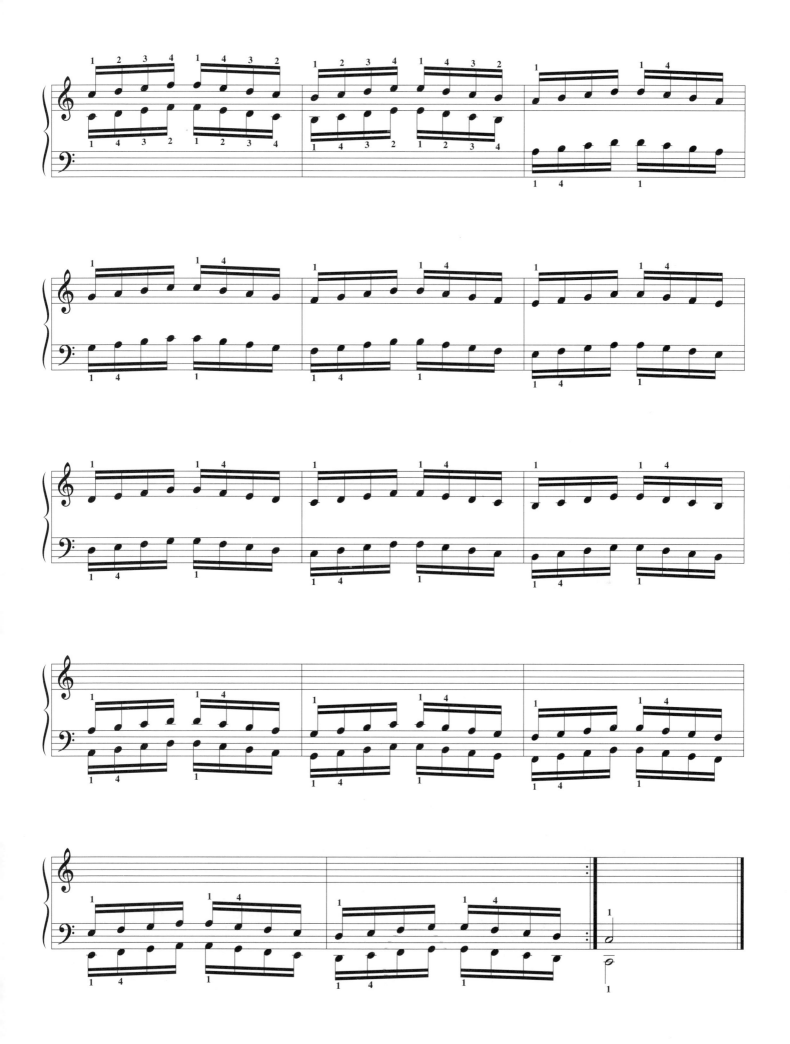

35

Turning the thumb under the 5th finger.

♩ = 40-72

Play this measure 10 times.

36

Another example of turning the thumb under.

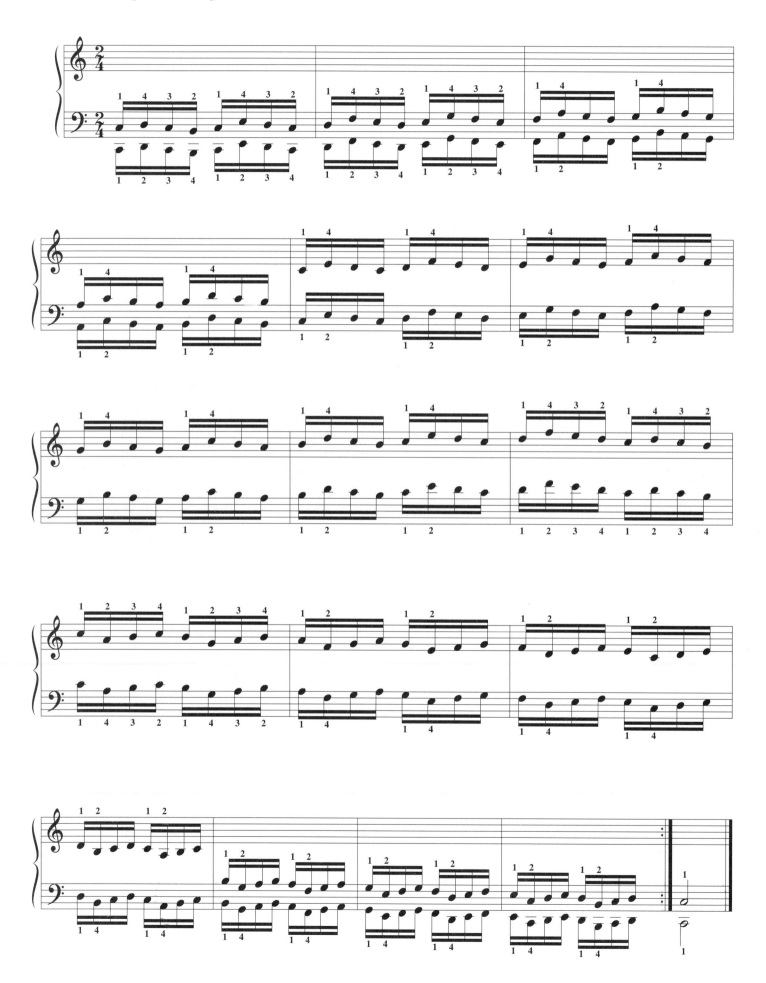

37

Special exercise for turning the thumb under.

Play this entire exercise with the two thumbs only.

(a) Hold down these three notes with each hand without striking them, while executing these 12 measures.

38

Preparatory exercise for the study of scales.

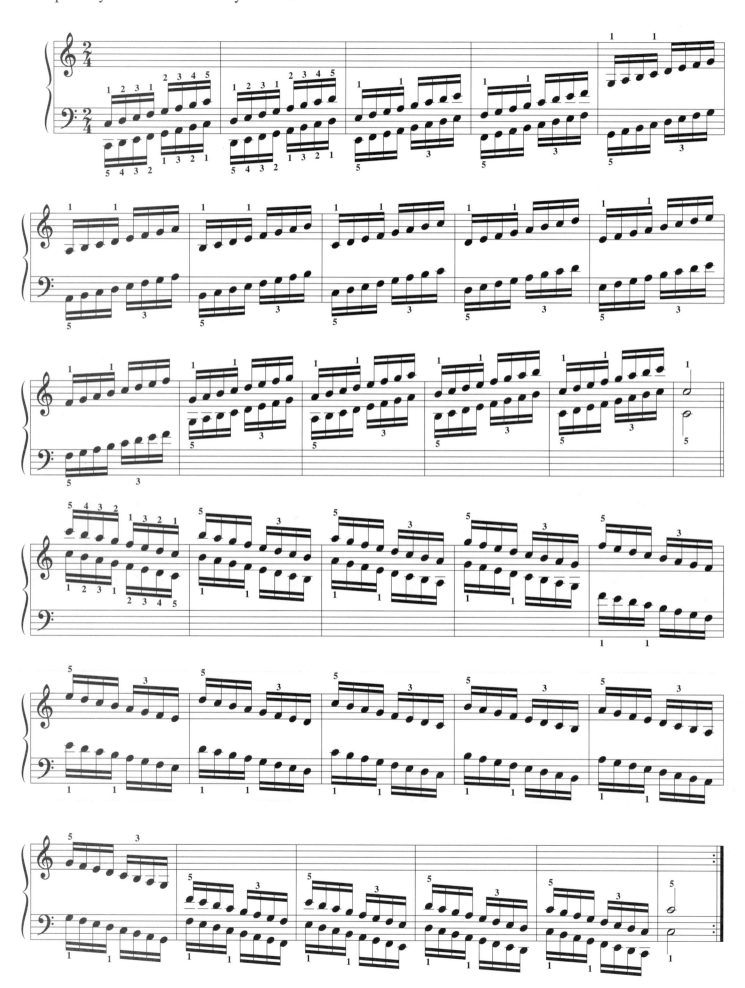

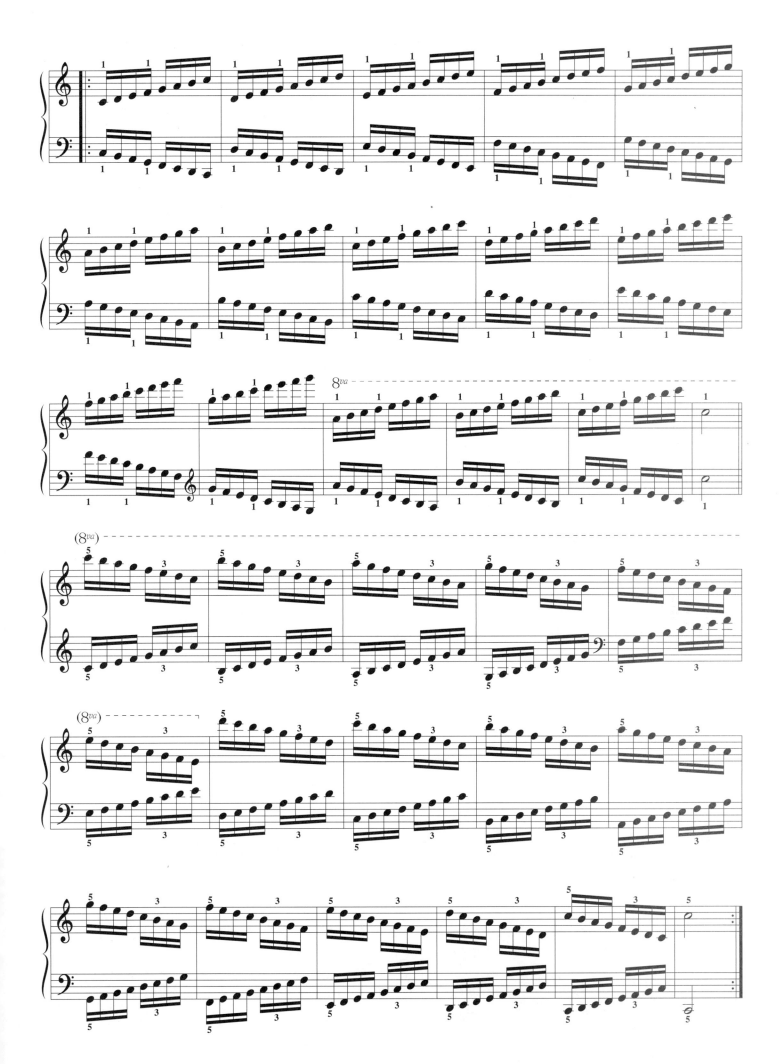

39
The 12 Major Scales and the 12 Minor Scales
Each major scale, followed by its relative minor

F major

1. D minor (harmonic)

2. D minor (melodic)

36

Bb major

1. G minor (harmonic)

2. G minor (melodic)

Eb major

1. C minor (harmonic)

2. C minor (melodic)

Ab major

1. F minor (harmonic)

2. F minor (melodic)

Db major

1. Bb minor (harmonic)

2. Bb minor (melodic)

Gb major

1. Eb minor (harmonic)

2. Eb minor (melodic)

B major

1. G♯ minor (harmonic)

2. G♯ minor (melodic)

E major

1. C# minor (harmonic)

2. C# minor (melodic)

A major

1. F♯ minor (harmonic)

2. F♯ minor (melodic)

D major

1. B minor (harmonic)

2. B minor (melodic)

G major

1. E minor (harmonic)

2. E minor (melodic)

40

Chromatic Scales

At the octave.
♩ = 60-120

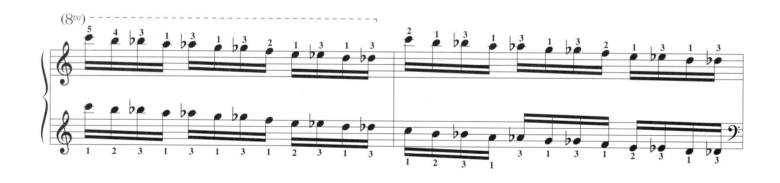

At the minor third.

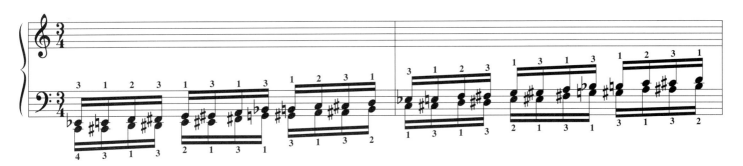

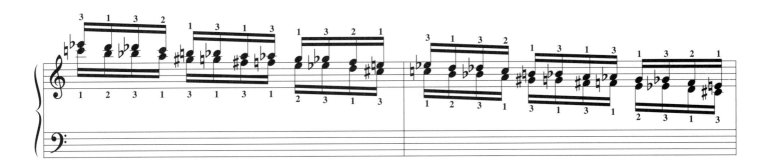

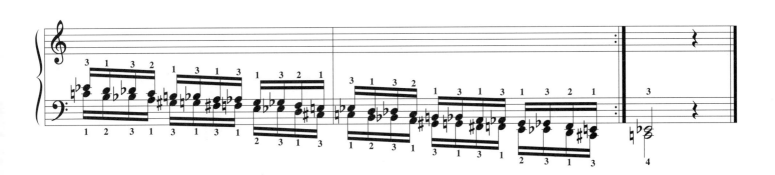

48

At the major sixth.

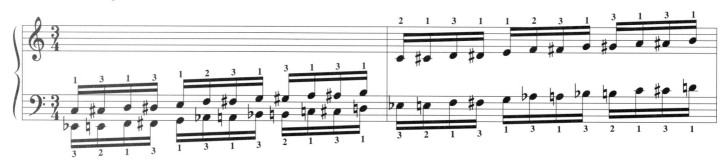

At the minor sixth.

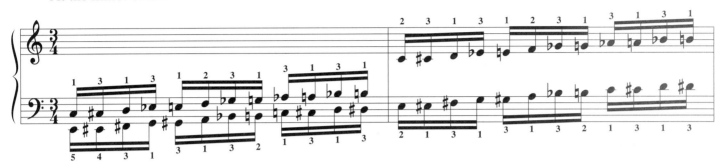

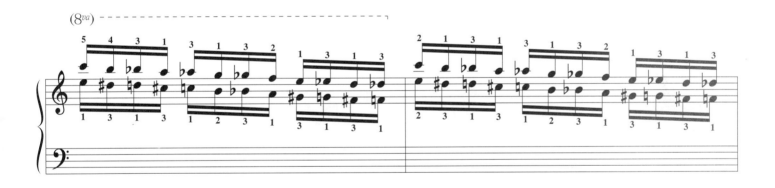

In contrary motion, beginning on the octave.

In contrary motion, beginning on the minor third.

In contrary motion, beginning on the major third.

Another fingering, which we particularly
recommend for legato passages.

41
Arpeggios on the Triads, in the 24 Keys

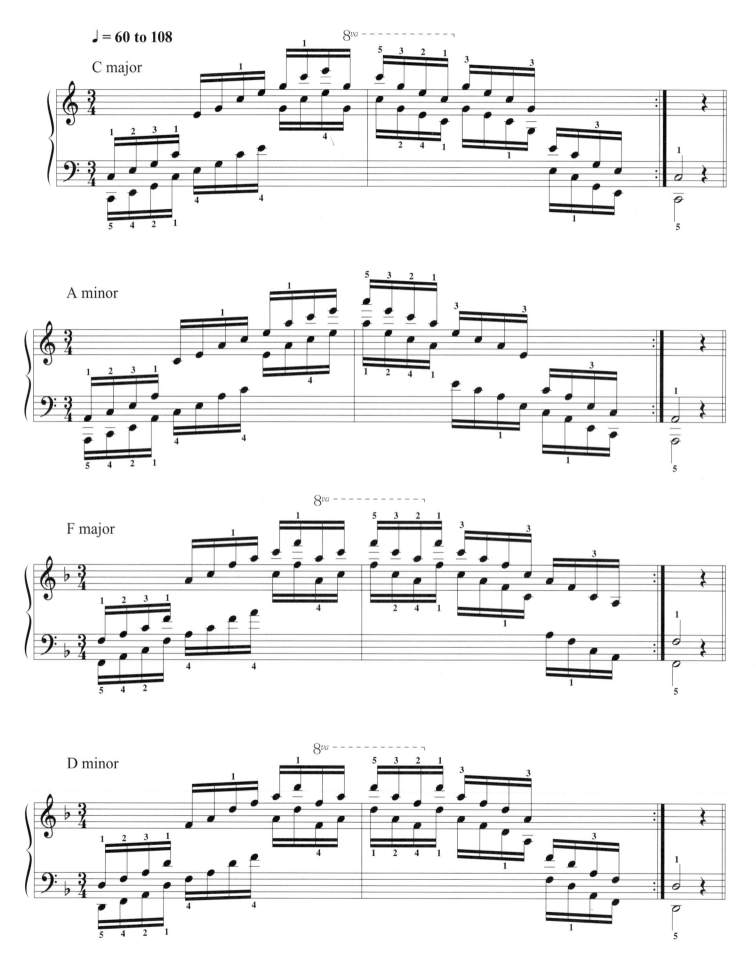

All 8ᵛᵃ's in Exercise 41 apply to both hands.

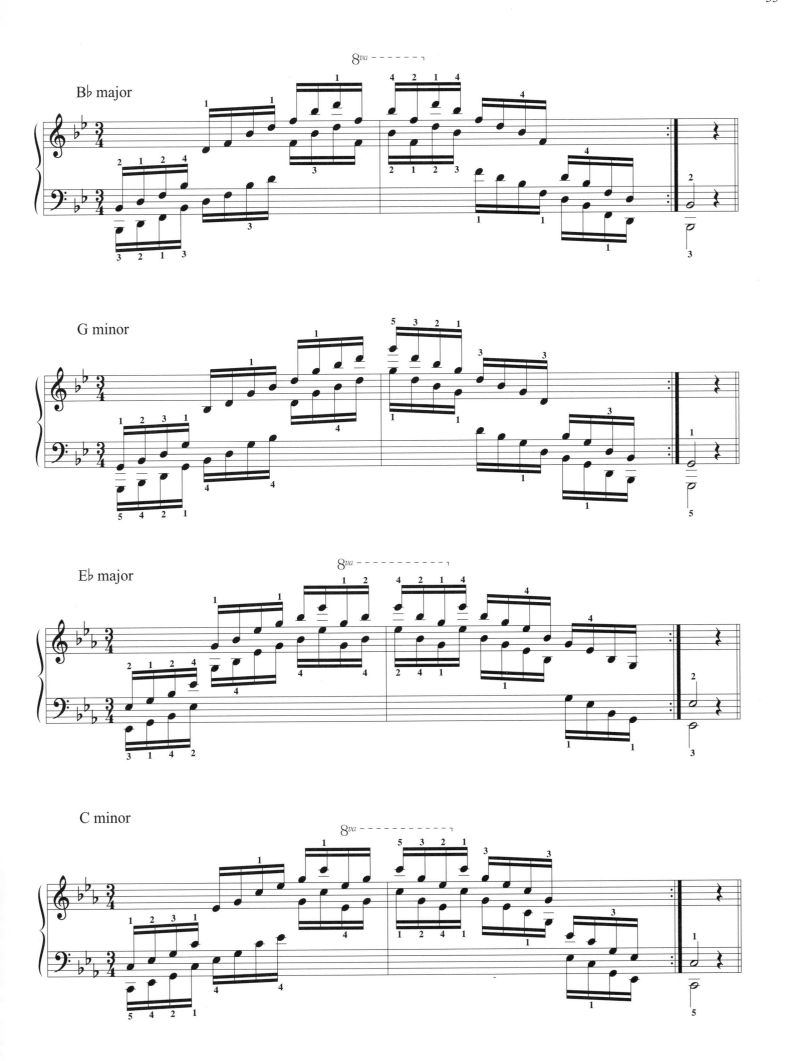

54

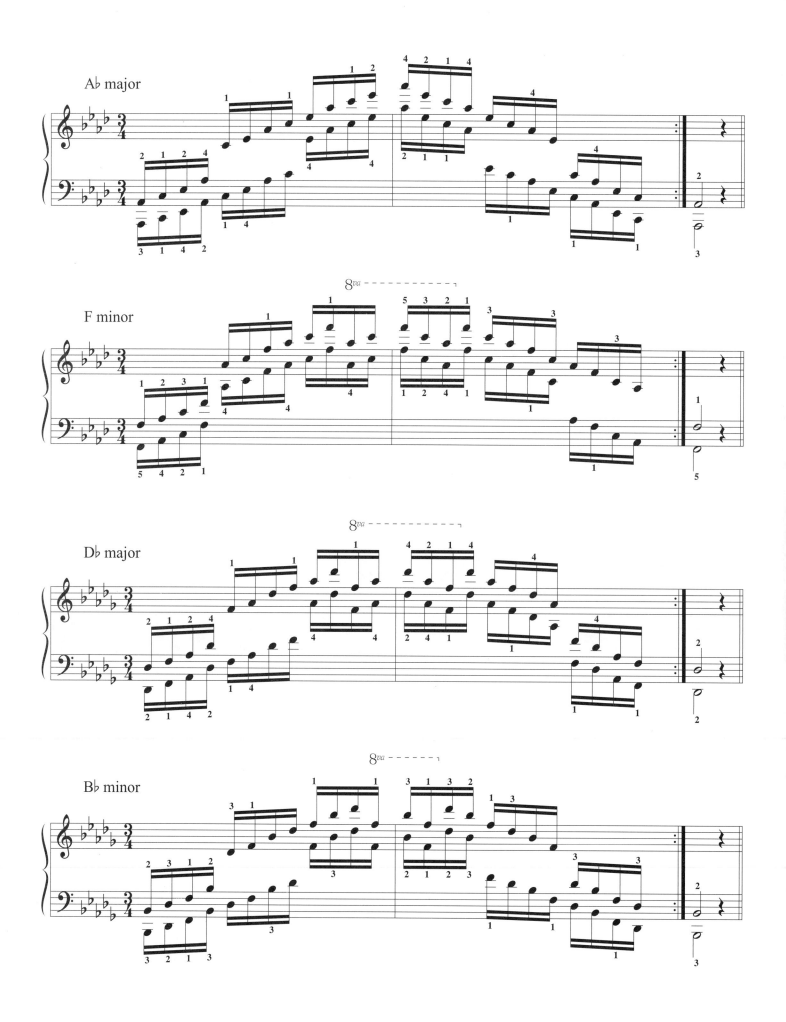

H1005

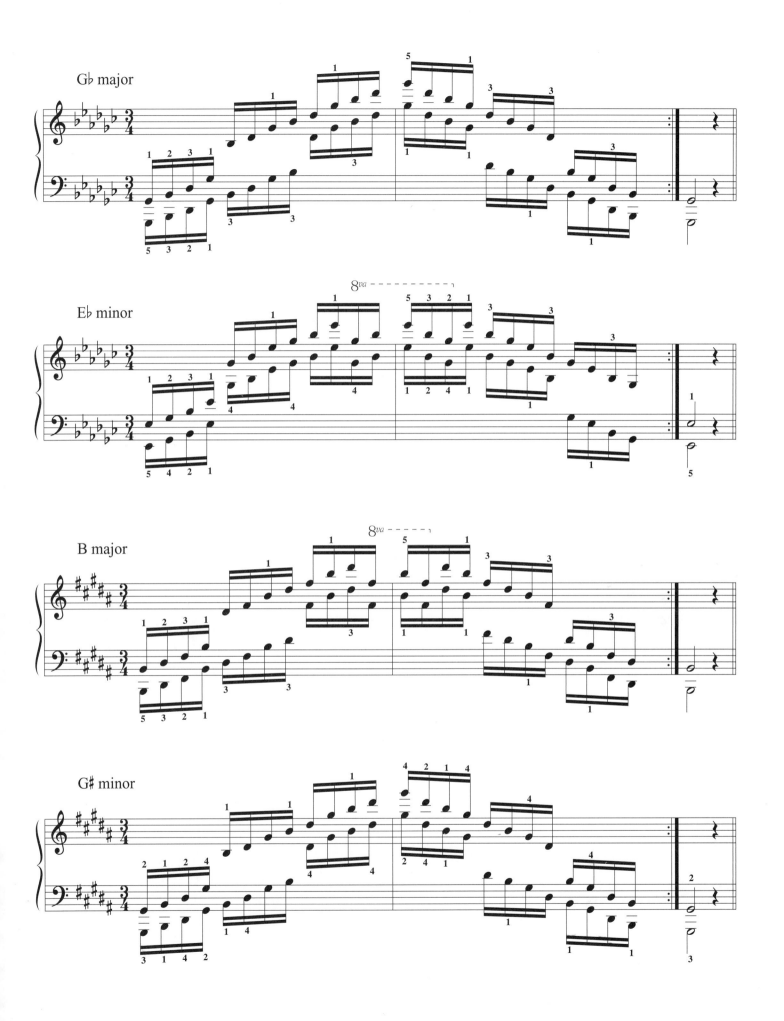

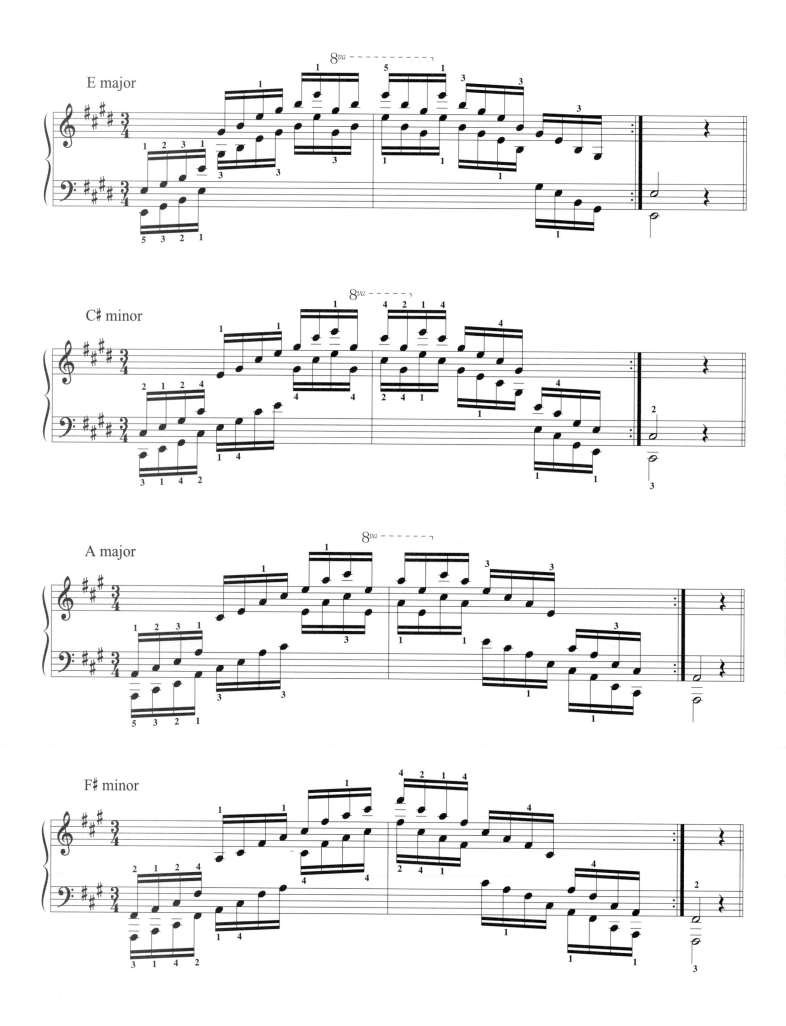

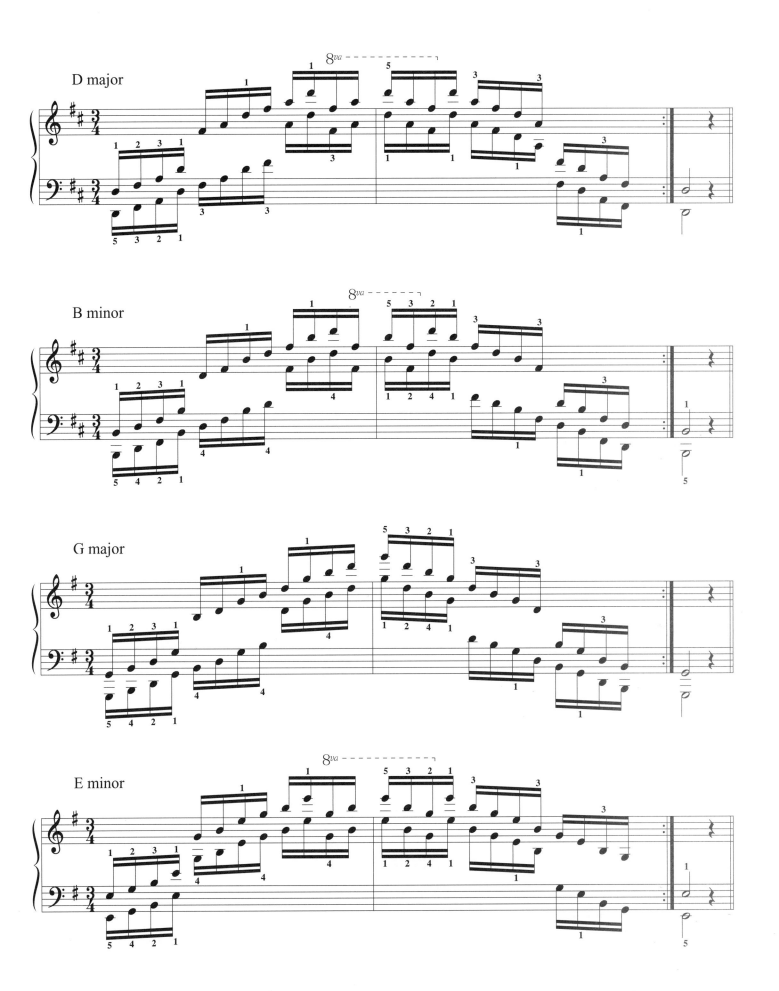

D major

B minor

G major

E minor

42
Extension (stretching) of the fingers
in chords of the diminished seventh, in arpeggios

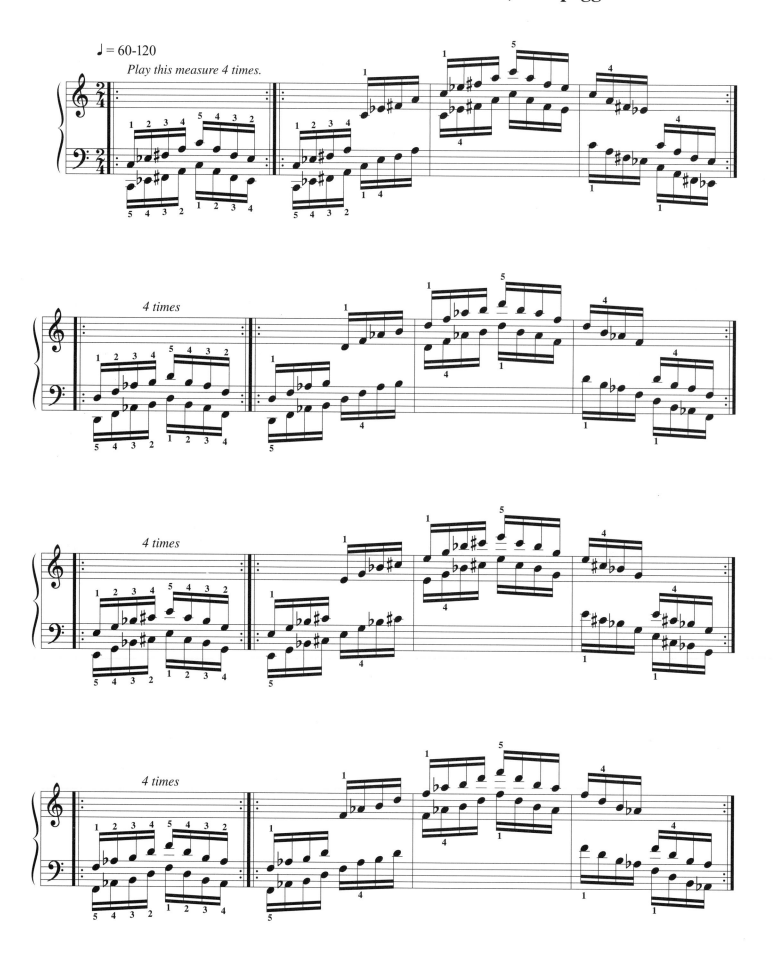

43

Extensions of the fingers in chords of the dominant seventh, in arpeggios.

♩ = 60 to 120

Play this measure 4 times.

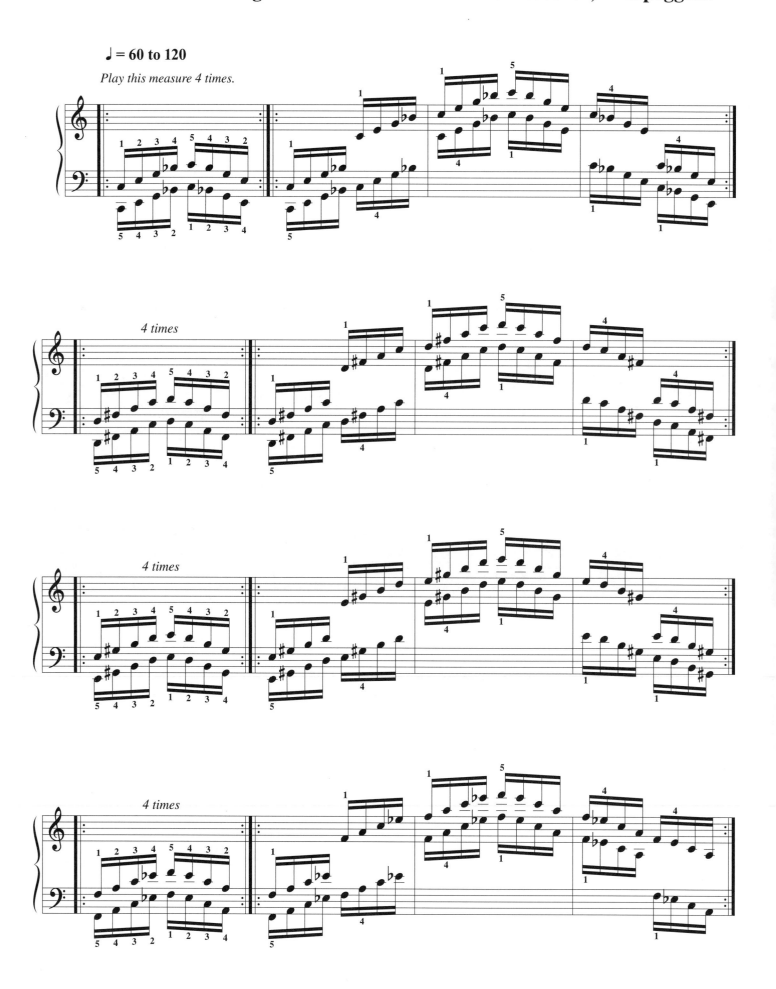

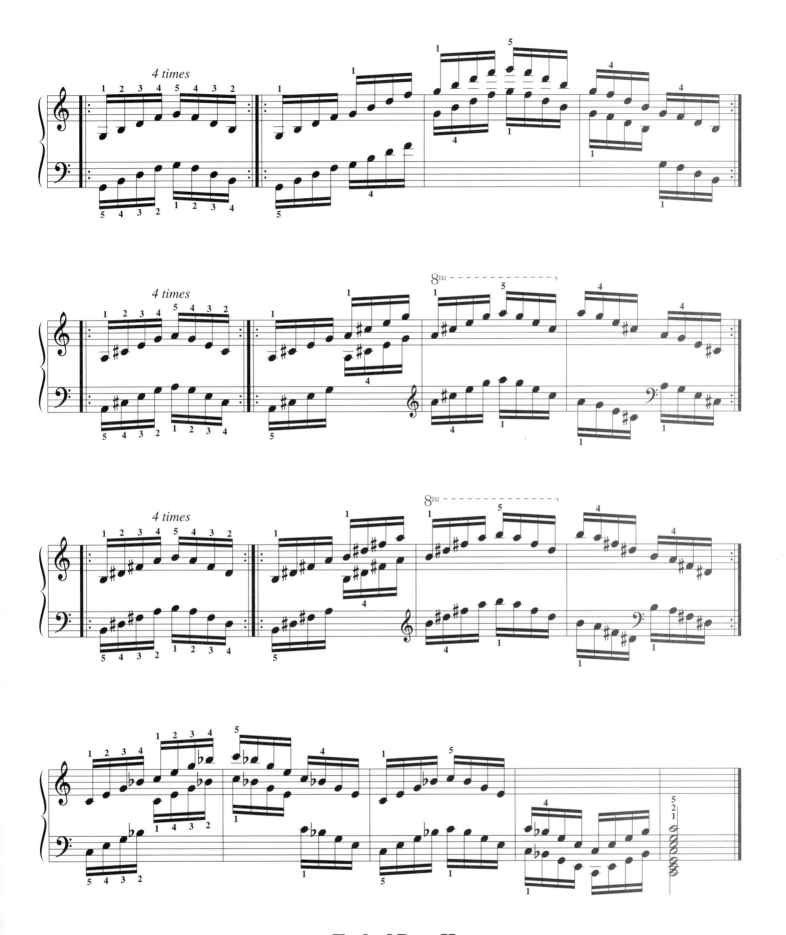

End of Part II.

Parts I and II of this work being the key to the difficulties in Part III, it is very important that they should be thoroughly mastered before commencing the virtuoso studies contained in Part III.